THE STORY OF BUDDHA

A Graphic Biography

THE STORY OF
BUDDHA
A Graphic Biography

By Hisashi Ota

THE STORY OF BUDDHA: A Graphic Biography
By Hisashi Ota
Published by Ichimannendo Publishing, Inc. (IPI)
970 West 190th Street, Suite 920, Torrance, California 90502
info@i-ipi.com   www.i-ipi.com
© 2011 by Hisashi Ota. All rights reserved.
Supervised by Kentaro Ito
Translated by Juliet Winters Carpenter

Jacket design by Kazumi Endo

First edition, December 2011
Printed in Japan
15 14 13 12 11   1 2 3 4 5 6 7 8 9 10

This book was originally published in Japanese by Ichimannendo Publishing under the title of
Manga de wakaru Buddha no ikikata.
© 2011 by Hisashi Ota

Distributed in the United States and Canada by Atlas Books Distribution, a division of
BookMasters, Inc.
30 Amberwood Parkway, Ashland, Ohio 44805
1-800-Booklog   www.atlasbooks.com

What is happiness?
What's the point of living the way I do, day in and day out?
Twenty-five hundred years ago, in his youth Buddha
(Śākyamuni) had the same nagging questions that we do today.
He never avoided them or gave up the search for answers, but
devoted himself earnestly to discovering the meaning of life.
That search is the starting point of Buddhism.
Precisely because he agonized more than others, Buddha also
attained a happiness greater than that of anyone else.
In our desire to live with strength and good cheer, the life of
Buddha is sure to provide invaluable insight.

Contents

Sites in the Life of Buddha

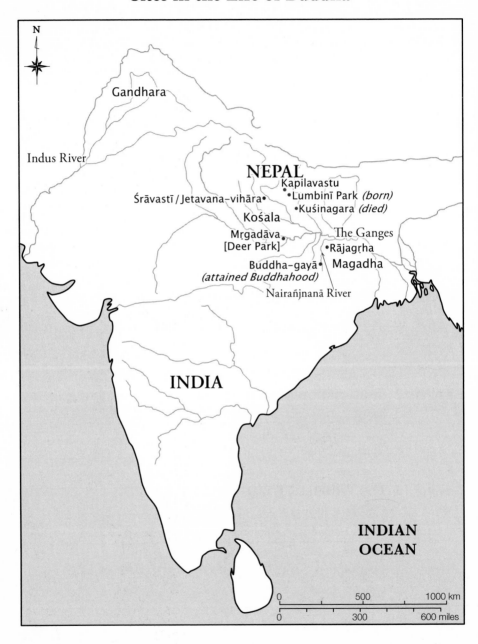

Some 2,500 years ago, near the present-day border between Nepal and India there was a great city called Kapilavastu, capital of the Śākya kingdom.

Everybody move! Clear the way!

The king and the crown prince are coming by.

1

Move, move!

Ow!

Don't have to be so rough . . .

Hey, aren't you Aśvajit?

Eh?

Well if it isn't Udda!

Still no job? A lady of leisure, eh?

Oh, be quiet.

Long time no see.

But I see you work in the palace now.

That's right. I'm in the service of Prince Siddhārtha.

Prince Siddhārtha . . .

Someday he'll be king and rule the land.

My future is set!

Anyway, I've got to get back to work.

See you!

Don't live off your parents forever, now!

Humph!

A young man who was raised in the Kapilavastu Palace later became the Buddha.

But at this point he was still only a youth full of questions, wondering about the purpose of life.

His name was Siddhārtha, and he was the crown prince.

Oh . . .

!

Ah . . . in the struggle to stay alive, living things kill and eat each other.

How pitiful . . .

They live in constant terror, never knowing when they may be attacked.

Where is the crown prince?

Next year I will expand the farmland over there, and . . .

Huh?

He was here a second ago . . .

What?

Don't just stand there, find him!

Y-Yes, Sire.

The crown prince is old enough to want to act on his own.

Hold your tongue!

Where could he have gone?

Huh? Is that . . .?

What is Siddhārtha doing?

He seems to be deep in thought.

He looks like an ascetic, one who has left home.

Left home, you say?

The king remembered a strange prediction made at his son's birth.

9

Well, what do you think of my newborn son, Siddhārtha!

Let me have a good look.

Oh, this child!

What is it?

This is no ordinary child.

What do you mean?

If he takes the throne, he will become a great monarch of the world.

Of the w-world?

And if he leaves home, he will attain the highest level of enlightenment.

Leaves home, you say?

Could the prophecy have been true?

A message for the king!

What's happening?

I bring word from the border garrison.

The army of the kingdom of Kośala is on the march, preparing to attack.

What!

They mean to strike during the festival, when people are making merry. Outrageous!

Hurry and prepare for war!

Father!

What is all this about?

My son! We are at war. Return to the palace.

Whenever you are ready, join the fray!

Yes, Sire!

Good grief. Time for planting, and all the young men are off to war!

Not again . . .

If the battle comes here, the fields will be trampled, and there'll be no crop.

Many will die. Only the old men will be left.

Our life is hard enough to begin with.

Ah . . .

We work and work, but never find ease.

I wonder.

What on earth will become of us?

Why do we have to go through such pain, just to live?

Ah! The law of the jungle isn't only for beasts.

Even among human beings, the strong prey on the weak in order to survive.

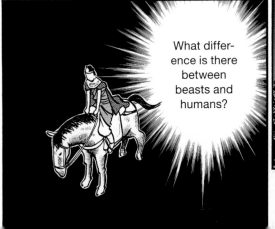

What difference is there between beasts and humans?

Even for royalty like me, with the country at war there is no telling when the end may come.

I live with that fear.

Why must we live in suffering and distress?

Why do we live?

Life is full of pain and anxiety . . .
so what is the point?

The palace

Chapter 2
Marriage to a Great Beauty

Siddhārtha was the firstborn son of King Śuddhodana

and his queen Mahāmāyā.

Soon after giving birth, Mahāmāyā died, and so Siddhārtha was raised by an aunt.

From childhood, Siddhārtha excelled at his studies and at martial arts.

Moreover, as crown prince his future was assured. He lacked for nothing in his daily life.

Yet in time he was tormented by the great question of life: Why do we live?

Nothing in the palace could satisfy his longings.

It's good that the recent border skirmish never turned serious.

Mm . . .

Is something wrong, Sire?

My son is depressed about something lately.

19

What can be on his mind?

Well, Sire . . .

I asked, but he would not tell me.

What more could he possibly want?

He leads a life that anyone would envy.

But, Sire . . .

Perhaps he wishes he had a woman to soothe his heart.

Hmm. I see.

Hahaha. Of course, that's it!

It's high time he took a wife.

All right, we'll find him the most beautiful girl in the kingdom.

Marriage should cure him of his troubles.

What's this parade for?

You don't know?

Prince Siddhārtha is getting married.

This is the bridal procession.

Oh really?

They say she's the most beautiful girl in the kingdom.

Oh my!

Then I could have been in the running, too!

Missed my chance.

Don't make me laugh.

You'd never rate a second glance.

Take that back!

Owww!

Sheesh.

Anyway, now the prince has everything a man could want. He must be perfectly happy.

I wonder.

The princess has arrived!

23

And so at age nineteen, Siddhārtha took the princess Yaśodharā as his wife.

With gentle Yaśodharā at his side, he embarked on peaceful wedded life.

Darling . . .

What are you looking at?

Oh, Yaśodharā, it's you.

Just look at all the stars in the sky.

So beautiful!

The sight of all these stars makes humans seem pretty insignificant, doesn't it?

......

People fight wars, expand their territory, win glory— but no one has ever conquered nature.

Compared to the grandeur of the Himalayas, we are like scurrying ants.

One day you will be king, ruler of this land.

How can you compare yourself to an ant?

Please don't say such depressing things.

What does an ant make of its life? We will never know.

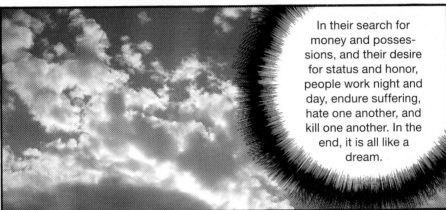

In their search for money and posses- sions, and their desire for status and honor, people work night and day, endure suffering, hate one another, and kill one another. In the end, it is all like a dream.

But that's the nature of life, is it not?

People do not live for the sake of living.

Think about it. Does anyone walk for the sake of walking?

The walker always has a goal in mind, a destination. Right?

......

Life too must have an ultimate purpose.

However painful, we must live life until that purpose has been fulfilled.

There has to be a purpose that can make us shout out when we finally achieve it, "This is what I was born for. I have no regrets in life."

What is that purpose? Why do we live?

Don't you want to know the answer, Yaśodharā?

Whatever
you may say,
I live for you.

Please don't
brood about
things so much.

Yaśodharā . . .

Now come in out of the night air. It's not good for you. Let's go to bed.

......

All right . . .

Look at the stars in the sky! . . .
Our lives seem so small in comparison.

The palace

What's this?

You want to spend more time outside the palace?

Yes, Father. I would like more opportunity to see nature and learn how the people live.

Hmm. One day you will rule this country.

It is not a bad idea for you to see society with your own eyes.

That will be better for you than moping around in your room.

......

Very well. Go and look around to your heart's content.

Thank you.

Chapter 3
The Four Gates: East Gate, South Gate

He has a beautiful wife, but he doesn't seem glad. Look at him.

I feel for Your Majesty.

Well, maybe this will help take his mind off his worries.

The East Gate of the palace

35

Prince Siddhārtha
…

Hmm?

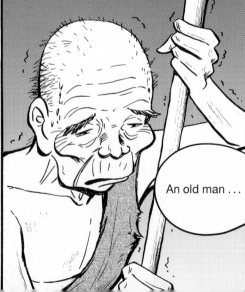

An old man . . .

Out of
the way,
you.
Move!

Why so
rough all
the time!

Stop that!

P-Prince
Siddhārtha!

I am sorry,
old man.

One of my
attendants was
inconsiderate.
I apologize.

Ah . . . kind
prince.

Please don't concern yourself about someone like me.

Old folks like me are just in the way.

Don't say that.

You must not talk like that. Stay strong and live your life!

See for yourself.

Oh . . . are they human?

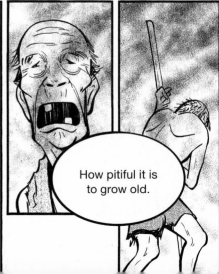

How pitiful it is to grow old.

Bent-backed and toothless, they can scarcely hobble around.

And on top of it all, they are treated as nuisances.

It's true even for young people like me. Year by year, age piles on.

The troubles of old age are inevitable. Is long life truly a blessing?

Prince Siddhārtha?

Tell me, why did you stand up for a decrepit old man like that?

That is the path we all must walk in our turn, is it not?

!!

Your Highness!

Please wait!

Welcome back, my love.

I have news.

I am pregnant.

Next spring I'll have a baby!

So I . . .

I see. Don't overdo, then.

I . . . but—

Wait . . .

I wonder what's the matter?

The South Gate of the palace

Who are they?

People who are seriously ill.

How very sad.

Can't anything be done?

Stop, Your Highness!

Pity them if you will, but you must keep your distance!

42

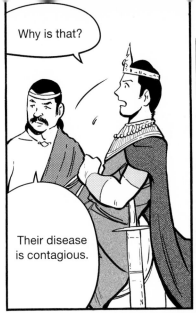

Why is that?

Their disease is contagious.

Anyone who goes near them will catch it, too.

It's a dreadful situation.

Husband, what has happened to you?

Just the other day you were fine . . .

Health may give way to sickness at any time. That is the reality of human life.

43

No one can escape sickness and pain.

I will go speak to the palace physician.

I will see that he provides them with medicine.

Your Highness, there is no reason to go to such extremes.

How can you turn a blind eye to suffering?

I-I . . .

Life is equally precious for all, regardless of station.

I want them to live their allotted life span to the end.

!?

What am I saying? Why go on living if it means struggling with old age and infirmity?

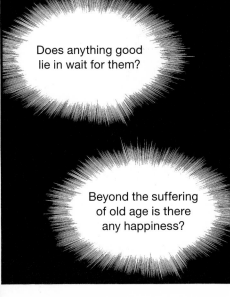

Does anything good lie in wait for them?

Beyond the suffering of old age is there any happiness?

Perhaps just encouraging people to hang on and live is irresponsible.

Y-Your Highness?

Unless life has an ultimate purpose whose attainment brings great joy, it can only end in suffering. The longer we live, it seems, the more suffering we must endure.

The troubles of sickness and old age are inevitable.
So is a long life really a blessing?

Siddhārtha.

I am planning to build a new palace soon, as a villa for myself.

Father, that is a huge undertaking.

Hahaha.

If you take the throne soon, then I can retire.

49

I want to sit back and enjoy the rest of my life.

Father, what are you saying! You, retire?

My son.

You must stop bothering about the meaning of life, and attend to your royal duties.

Chapter 4
The Four Gates: West Gate

......

Harrumph.

Siddhārtha, you take life too seriously.

No, Father, all I want to know is how to achieve true happiness.

The answer is simple.

Build a fortune, elevate your status, and rule the people wisely.

Then spend your days in pleasure. What is wrong with that?

Son!

What to do with him . . .

The West Gate
of the palace

52

What have
we here?

A funeral procession.

There must have
been a death in
a neighboring
village.

Funeral?

Your Highness!

A cemetery . . . how lonely and sad it is here.

Your Highness, this is no place for you.

Did someone die again today?

?

Let us go home now.

'Yesterday there was a funeral.' Those who say so are not long for this world either.

Who are you?

I live here.

They call me a grave keeper.

Spooky.

Old man, do you observe people's deaths here every day?

That was a woman from the edge of town.

She lived alone. They found her three days after she died.

Ugh!

Oh no . . .

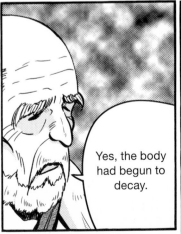

Yes, the body had begun to decay.

In her youth she was the prettiest girl in town, and everyone admired her. How pitiful she should end this way . . .

Stop that creepy talk!

Leave him be.

Old man, continue.

Over there is the village head.

He worked himself to death to make money, but when he died, he left all his fortune behind.

Over there is someone who became desperately ill and recovered, over and over again, only to die anyway in the end.

All people

must die in the end . . .

Something good will happen, so live with all your might. Life is good, I was told. I have lived for so many years.

But what is waiting at the end of my life?

Look at the scene before you.

Status and possessions earned by the sweat of your brow are all left behind.

Death means parting from wife and children, too.

The other day, children and babies were buried here.

There is no guarantee that old people will always die first!

Your Highness, there you are no different from anyone else.

58

No, he's right. People live in search of happiness, but in fact life leads straight to the horror of the grave.

It is absolutely true.

How dare you!

What could be more contradictory?

Is my life too a mere prelude to death?

If so, then life has no meaning whatsoever.

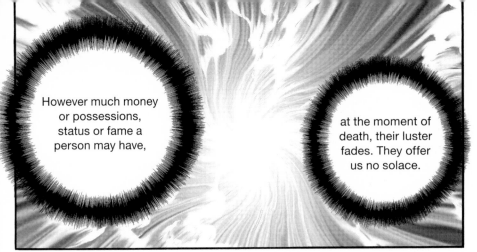

However much money or possessions, status or fame a person may have,

at the moment of death, their luster fades. They offer us no solace.

Whoa!

Father, is it right for a man to live only for pleasure?

Is it right to live in a fog, never thinking of life's ultimate purpose?

We live but once, and if we die with regret, there is no remedy.

What should I do with myself?

I want to know the meaning of life!

Death comes without warning.
However much money or possessions, status or fame a person
may have, at the moment of death, their luster fades.
They offer us no solace.

The North Gate of the palace

Prince Siddhārtha, lately you have been looking a bit pale.

......

The king is hoping that this excursion will help you to forget your troubles.

Try to find peace of mind.

Peace of mind . . .

That's it.

Chapter 5
The Four Gates: North Gate

Your Highness, what you need is a hobby you can lose yourself in with pleasure.

A hobby?

Yes, Your Highness.

You might not know it to look at me, but I enjoy giving musical performances.

Do you, now?

When I go home, I am always practicing.

Well, well ... who would have guessed it?

I have mastered some fairly difficult pieces.

Throwing myself into my music feels good.

It helps me to forget whatever is weighing me down.

A scolding from the king, say, or a meeting with an unpleasant minister.

Haha. So my father scolds you, too, does he?

Oops.

P-please forgive me for speaking out of turn.

Never mind. I understand perfectly.

Some people say that happiness lies in giving in to the flow of things.

But the pleasure to be gained from hobbies and other pursuits is only temporary.

Beg pardon?

When you finish performing, are you not plunged straight back into reality?

The next day you must return to work . . .

. . . meet with the minister you dislike . . .

. . . perhaps be scolded again by the king.

That is certainly true.

......

When that happens, does the music you played the day before still have power to make you happy?

Such troubles are far from the worst.

Outside the gates to the east, south, and west, I have seen people beset by old age, people suffering from illness, people headed to the grave.

None of us can escape the realities of old age, sickness, and death.

I want to know something more fundamental.

Why people live, and what true happiness is: this is what I want to know.

Ah, yes.

Psst, help me out here!

Who, me? This is way over my head!

Darned if I know.

Mm?

Who is that?

That is an ascetic.

An ascetic?

Yes. Someone who leaves home and goes into the mountains for intense spiritual training.

I could never do such a thing.

Your Highness.

I beg your pardon . . .

73

May I ask what you seek to gain from asceticism?

I want to learn the root of human suffering . . .

By so doing, I want to be freed from suffering and gain true ease.

!

The root of human suffering?

Thinking about that will only drag you down.

Instead of practicing austerities, why not lose yourself in the pleasure of doing what you want?

That is exactly like getting drunk on wine.

While you are drunk you may enjoy yourself, but only for a short time. Drunkenness solves nothing.

If you truly relish life, there is no need to mask your pain and loneliness with wine.

......

I want to be able to shout out how wonderful it is to be alive.

I want to know life's ultimate purpose, and attain it.

Then surely each moment of my life would outshine the stars in the heavens.

What a weirdo.

Surely this is the path I need to take.

This is it!

Y-Your Highness?

I want to be able to shout out with joy,
"How wonderful it is to be alive!"

Your Highness?

Your Highness! Your Highness!

Congratulations, Your Highness.

What's all this?

Princess Yaśodharā has given birth to a prince.

Wow!

Is it true?

How wonderful! Congratulations!

Please accept our sincere congratulations.

Th-Thank you.

Let us return to the palace immediately. The princess will be anxious to see you.

Um, right.

The palace

Oh, Siddhārtha! Hurry in here!

It's a gem of a baby boy.

I-I am happy to hear it.

Well done, well done! Now the royal line is safe.

Now I can retire without a care in the world!

No, Father, it is too soon for you to retire.

Hahaha.

Anyway, now more than ever you need to devote yourself to affairs of state.

In my search for life's true meaning, this child may become a *rāhula* [hindrance] . . .

Rāhula?

83

Based on the prince's murmured aside, the child was named Rāhula.

Come on, son! Show your wife a little more consider-ation, will you!

Hahaha.

Behind the facade of happiness in palace life, the prince's anxiety only deepened.

What is it, Aśvajit?

Hm? Oh, it's you, Udda.

You seem a little down.

Not feeling well?

No, I'm fine.

It's Prince Siddhārtha.

He has a beautiful consort and an heir, and one day he will be king.

Is something wrong with the prince?

It is everything anyone could wish for, yet he seems not to enjoy life much at all.

I just don't get it.

Huh.

He just needs to let loose a little . . .

I think it shows that money and possessions can't bring true happiness.

R-Really?

Oh yes.

Obtaining happiness is really not so simple after all, is it?

Huh.

Anyway, the king is so worried that he has decided to build the prince a palace for each season of the year.

Each season?

Yes.

And he'll have 500 beauties to entertain him.

500?!

Yes. Lucky him.

......

What is it, Udda?

Do you suppose I could be one of the 500?

You? Don't be crazy!

Why not? You have connections. Couldn't you arrange it for me?

This is it . . .

Hmm . . . maybe becoming a court lady would be better than hanging around doing nothing, at that.

I'll put in a good word for you.

Thanks!

89

Money and possessions cannot bring us true happiness.

Your Highness, look!

Rare fruits from a far-off southern land.

Fine wine with a deep flavor that can make you forget all your cares.

Won't you try some?

Never mind fruit and wine!

Come have some fun with me!

Hehehe.

The girls are doing a fine job.

Sire, isn't this going a bit overboard?

Besides the most beautiful woman in the kingdom as his wife, giving him 500 beauties and a palace . . .

What's wrong with that?

Wine and women are the best cure for any man's troubles.

Yes, but . . . what will the people think?

There are bound to be scoffers.

Let them scoff.

The prince's excursions out the four palace gates seem only to have deepened his concerns about life.

I want him to put all that behind him and enjoy life.

As his father, that is all I ask of him now.

You must understand.

Yes, Sire.

Siddhārtha!

I don't know what you are unhappy about.

You need to think of your position!

You are destined to become king of this country!

95

Your Highness looks unhappy.

You find our company tiresome?

What?

N-No . . .

That's not it . . .

In that case . . .

Status, possessions, brains, family, beautiful women . . .

Your Highness has everything a person could ever want, and at such a young age!

What more could you possibly ask for?

It is certainly true that I lack for nothing material.

But sooner or later, my life will come to an end.

......

I don't want to waste my life in the pursuit of pleasure.

What is the best way to live a truly wonderful life with no regrets?

Your Highness, that kind of talk has no place here!

She's right.

See, you've spoiled the mood.

......

Look at us.

All we need to do now is shake things up and have fun!

Woo!

That is the purpose of living from moment to moment!

The reason you want to make merry is because otherwise your life is dreary.

!

Don't you ever stop to wonder why life requires such effort?

Wha . . .

Why bother about the purpose of life? Life is more fun if you forget about such things!

Ohoho-hoho!

Come now, Your Highness. Watch us dance.

Start the music!

Tee-hee.

We'll chase away all your nasty blues!

How happy-go-lucky they are!

And yet . . .

Seeing everyone else act this way makes me feel peculiar for brooding so much.

Your Highness, you must be thirsty.

Hm?

Please help yourself.

Well, thank you.

I haven't seen you before. What is your name?

My name is Udda.

Your Highness, I—

Hey!

A serving girl has no business talking to His Highness so familiarly!

Who does she think she is?

I'm sorry.

Come dance with us.

Give me your hand, Your Highness!

Fine wine and beautiful women bring no lasting peace.
The emptiness of life cannot be filled by pleasure.

The Palaces of the Seasons

Oh—

Where are you going, Your Highness?

Out to relieve myself, that's all.

Chapter 8
Three Wishes

My son.

How goes it?
Enjoying the
party?

Father . . .

Hahaha.

You have done well, my son.

In your studies and in the martial arts, you have surpassed your teachers.

Not at all . . .

The greatest scholar in the land declared he has nothing left to teach you.

So now you can relax and enjoy yourself.

All right?

Thank you for your concern, father.

Do you still fear that my anxiety will cause me to leave home?

This is my way of rewarding you.

What ...?

Is that why you are trying to distract me?

With beautiful women galore and a lavish table, what more could you need?

What I want is something else.

Wh-What is it? If there is anything you want, say the word.

I have three wishes.

Don't hold out on me, Siddhārtha.

Father . . .

What are they?

I will see that they come true, so tell me.

First, I want you to prevent me from ever growing old.

Second, I want you to see that I never take sick.

Third, please see to it that I never die.

Wh-What?!

If you can grant these three wishes of mine, I will not leave home.

D-Don't talk craziness! That's impossible and you know it!

Old age, sickness and death take away all our happiness.

I want real happiness—the kind that will make me rejoice that I was born human!

Father!

Siddhārtha, don't talk madness.

Have you no inkling of my fatherly concern for you?

Act more like a member of this royal family!

Your Highness!

Welcome back.

While you were gone, we were so lonely!

Come here!

Leave me alone.

Eh?

112

I want to be alone. You are all excused.

Wh-What's wrong, Your Highness?

Enough! I'm telling you to leave.

At once!

......

I wonder what the trouble is?

Something or other was not to his liking.

Let's go home for today.

His Highness is handsome, but kind of prickly, isn't he?

I have nowhere to go.

No home? No parents?

My parents have no need of me, so I'm as good as an orphan.

How so?

I was dis-obedient.

I didn't apply myself to my work.

I just fooled around . . .

My parents disowned me and threw me out of the house.

Oh no!

Then my sweetheart left me. I have been living in a daze . . .

No one needs me. I wish I had never been born.

Y-You mustn't say such a thing.

I'm useless, like trash.

No, no, you must value your life!

Why is that, Your Highness?

But . . .

I beg of you, please tell me.

Tell me the meaning of life, Your Highness!

118

Promise me freedom from old age, sickness, and death,
and I will abandon my quest.

Why must people live, and never take their own lives?

121

Tell me the meaning of life!

I had no proper answer to her earnest questions.

I spend all my time thinking about the meaning of life, yet when someone asks me about it, I have no reply.

Chapter 9
Out of the Palace and into the Mountains

A fine state of affairs!

Your Highness!

Would you like some more wine?

Y-Yes.

This is more like it!

This fine wine is just right for a noble prince like you!

Whew.

I never knew wine tasted so good . . .

Somehow it makes me forget all my uncertainties and cheer up.

Finally you have come to appreciate the taste of wine!

That shows that now you are an adult.

I-It does?

Yes, Your Highness.

And it makes me very happy.

Here you are.

Let me pour some too!

Hahaha.

Everyone, drink up!

How wonderful!

Drink and dance, everyone!

Your Highness, we will show you the time of your life!

Cheers!

Hahaha.

It's not so bad to lay aside questions about human suffering and lead a carefree life.

Forgetting hard questions and losing oneself in pleasure may offer a kind of salvation . . .

Ow, my head.

Urgh.

I feel sick. Hung over . . .

Zzz

Huh?

I must have fallen asleep.

Snooore

Peering through the darkness, the prince saw the women lying disheveled in sleep, completely unlike their daytime selves.

What on earth?

Skznkk

Can these be those bewitching women?!

A fine sight this is.

People decorate themselves on the outside to cover up the ugliness within.

The way these women are now shows people's true nature.

The pleasure of satisfying one's desires is intense, but it cannot last.

This was not the answer to suffering!

I cannot stay here a moment longer!

I have wasted precious time . . .

Wake up!

Hmngh

Y-Your Highness!?

Sh!

I am leaving the palace.

Prepare my horse without letting anyone know.

S-So late at night, Your Highness?

130

Yaśodharā . . .

If I pick up the baby to say goodbye, Yaśodharā will surely wake up and try to stop me from going . . .

Your Highness.

You mean to leave the palace, don't you?

Udda.

I came close to running away from your question.

Why must we live, though we suffer? I must find the answer.

......

Here in the palace no one thinks of the meaning of life, no one tries to search it out. It is not an issue here.

Yet nothing is so baffling.

Here I can never hope to understand.

Everyone in the palace will be shocked and saddened if you leave.

I know.

But if I find the answer to life's most basic problem—the answer to the question "Why live?"—then I can share it with everyone.

That will lead not only to my happiness but also to the happiness of my father and Yaśodharā . . .

. . . and all of you as well.

Your Highness . . .

Take good care of yourself.

Udda, I will be back. I promise.

Wait for me.

Oh!

Your Highness!

134

This happened on February 8, when Siddhārtha was 29 years old.

Why do we live? Finding the answer to this question is the key to lasting happiness.

I am going to become an ascetic.

You return to the palace.

Your Highness, you are leaving home after all!

Do not be so sad.

People are tied by feelings of love and devotion, but in the end old age, sickness, and death lead inevitably to parting.

Chapter 10
The Five Messengers

And to suffering.

Why must we go on living, no matter how painful our life is?

I will not return until I have found the answer— the purpose of life.

Your Highness.

Give my regards to my father the king.

Your Highness—!!

Your Highness!

First I will call on a renowned ascetic and learn from him.

The palace

What! The prince has left, you say!

140

With all these people here, how could no one have noticed!!

Who would have thought the prince and you would have such a conversation!

......

The whole palace is in an uproar.

The king is beside himself, and Princess Yaśodharā has taken to her bed with grief.

It's all right. He is sure to be back.

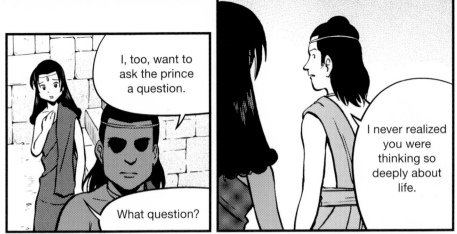

I, too, want to ask the prince a question.

What question?

I never realized you were thinking so deeply about life.

I never understood the prince's distress, either.

143

I always thought it was enough in life to try to get everything you could ever want. You know, to satisfy your every desire.

But now I've finally come to see things differently.

That sort of life can never be fulfilling.

I feel like I've forgotten something important . . .

Don't look at me that way.

Maybe if I tell His Highness you've been in the dumps ever since he left, he'll come right back.

Just a minute, Aśvajit!

Ha ha! See you!

You must find the prince, is that clear?

Yes, Sire.

Kauṇḍinya

I will persuade him to change his mind and bring him back to the palace without fail.

145

Good. I'm counting on you.

We're off!

Husband ...

What is the
point of
human life?

What should we
truly seek, why
do we live?

Don't you
want to know,
Yaśodharā?

My husband!!

I have news!

Over in that village I found someone who met the prince!

Ah! And then?

Apparently he went to call on a famed ascetic.

They say he is engaged in ascetic practice deep in the mountains to the east.

All right, let's be off.

Giddyup!

Make it quick.

I am sorry to say that Siddhārtha left here.

W-Why did he go?

I had nothing more to tell him.

Never have I encountered anyone so quick in understanding.

......

C-Can you tell us where he went?

Let me see . . .

I believe he left here in search of true enlighten- ment.

Deep in a forest far to the south.

Thank you.

OK

Let's go!!

150

Prince Siddhārtha!

What the—?

Look at him!

Your Highness, it's me, Kauṇḍinya. I have come for you.

I beg of you, come back with me to the palace.

You traveled a long way.

You must have come on my father's orders.

You have done enough. Turn around and go back.

No, Your Highness! I cannot give up so easily.

Ever since you left, the palace has been deep in mourning.

Princess Yaśodharā weeps morning and night, and cannot eat.

154

The king is so distracted by worry that he cannot attend to affairs of state.

All your retainers and the whole nation are eagerly awaiting your return!

I beg of you, hear me!

The search party conveyed King Śuddhodana's impassioned message, and with tears implored the prince to reconsider.

Please do not make me say it again.

Nothing can shake my resolve.

Now go on back to the palace.

Your Highness, are you that determined?

Agh, what can I do?

Your Highness.

I heard from Udda about what is in your heart.

You know her?

Yes. We were childhood chums.

There is something I long to ask you.

What is it?

I have heard that there are four reasons why people leave home on a spiritual quest.

One is a prolonged illness that inter-feres with the pleasure of life.

Another is old age, which takes away one's freedom of movement and hope for the future.

Another is the loss of money, possessions, and livelihood.

Also there is grief at the death of a loved one— sadness at the brevity of life.

But none of these reasons applies to Your Highness.

You are young and in superb physical condition.

You can live in a splendid palace with your fine consort and heir. You have everything a man could want.

He's right.

Everyone in the kingdom has reason to envy you.

And yet, and yet . . .

How could you leave all that behind to seek enlightenment in a distant place?

He's right again. It makes no sense to me.

I cannot under-stand Your Highness's way of thinking.

Why not do your spiritual practices in the palace, if you must?

I implore you, please return to the palace with us.

I beg of you!

159

Your Highness.

Your Highness!

......

What?

Do you not understand?

......

162

In the face of the prince's fiery resolve, the five messengers were helpless.

Why can't you understand?
Nothing in this world is permanent.

The palace

How dare you come crawling back empty-handed!

Sire, I am very sorry.

Where is my son, Prince Siddhārtha!

His Highness's resolve was far greater than we had imagined.

Chapter 11
Ascetic Practices

We pleaded with him over and over, but to no avail.

Hmm . . .

Wh-What did my son have to say?

He said this, Sire.

What is the ultimate cause of suffering in human life?

Once I ascertain the truth, a life of supreme joy will become possible not only for me but for all people.

Until I have clarified the root of suffering, and found the solution, I cannot possibly return to the palace.

His determination is that strong, is it?

Yes, Sire, unfortunately.

......

168

Then you five join Siddhārtha in his asceticism.

Sire, what are you saying?

Are you telling us to leave home as well?

Yes. While you're at it, you can see to the prince's various needs.

S-Sire . . .

He has spent his whole life in the royal palace. Living on his own is sure to pose many difficulties.

At this point, this is all I can do for Siddhārtha as his father.

169

Please understand.

Yes, Sire!

I, Kauṇḍinya, swear to carry out His Majesty's order!

Me too!

All right. I am counting on you.

Your Majesty . . .

Oh, Yaśodharā!

Here are some clothing and some food supplies.

Princess Yaśodharā!

The rations will all keep a long time.

Please take them along.

Princess . . .

Protect His Highness!

That is all I ask.

Yes, Your Highness!

I cannot turn away any who wish to undergo spiritual training.

Th-Thank you, Your Highness.

We brought food and clothing from your royal father and your wife.

Those I must reject. I have no need of them.

But Your Highness . . .

I understand how they feel.

I gratefully accept their warm concern.

I am undertaking austerities at the risk of my life.

I cannot accept anything from you.

Wh-Wha . . .

W-What understanding can lie beyond such extreme self-mortification?

GULP

The ancient texts reveal that Siddhārtha's austerities included a restricted diet, fasting, breath control, special ways of sitting and standing, and more. In this way he strengthened his control over his own flesh, and toughened his spirit.

174

And yet . . .

In the search for enlightenment, I have pushed my body to the limit and beyond.

But all I am doing is weakening myself in body and mind.

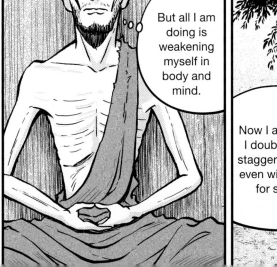

Now I am so weak I doubt if I could stagger to my feet, even with this tree for support.

Unless I recover my physical and mental strength, I cannot achieve true insight.

You have come a long way in your spiritual training.

It's strange . . . I came here on the king's orders to attend to the prince's needs, never dreaming I too would take up the life of an ascetic.

I am nowhere near your equal, Kauṇḍinya.

The prince is committed so deeply to unimaginable austerities that he spurns all the things we brought.

Yes, that is true . . .

I myself have come to want to seek truth more wholeheartedly.

I feel the same way.

I want to devote myself to training and somehow gain enlightenment.

Me too.

You do too, do you?

But the prince is amazing.

We'd never be able to go through such rigorous austerities.

Huh?

Your Highness . . .

179

Where could he be going in that condition?

First I need to cleanse my body of all its accumulated grime.

Look! His Highness!

Bathing himself . . .

What on earth is he thinking?

In his condition it's not safe to go in the river.

We've got to bring him back!

Wait!

There's something strange about him.

Let's keep an eye on him.

181

Urghh...

Look!

He isn't strong enough to pull himself onto the bank.

Wait!!

Someone is coming.

Sujāhtā

Oh, no!

Someone has collapsed!

Hello . . . are you all right?

Ungh . . .

I have been undergoing austerities in the forest near here.

You have nothing to fear from me.

I am from a nearby village.

I'll go fetch help.

No.

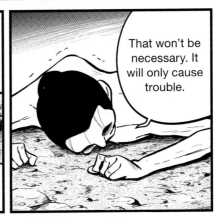

That won't be necessary. It will only cause trouble.

If you would be so kind, could you give me something to eat?

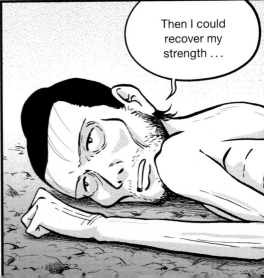

Then I could recover my strength . . .

Here, have this milk rice.

The food from Sujāhtā gave the prince new strength, and finally he was able to pull himself ashore.

I-I don't believe my eyes!

The prince couldn't endure the austerities, and became depraved!

Imagine that! An ascetic approaching a woman.

At this rate he will never, ever gain enlightenment!

If we follow him, we too will become depraved.

No, that can't be true.

His Highness must have a reason for his actions.

Be quiet!

You saw him beg for food from a woman!

How can I possibly follow the prince anymore?

I'm leaving! Let's get out of here!

Me too. This is disgusting.

The men turned their backs on Prince Siddhārtha and went off to the west.

187

Until I have clarified the root of suffering, and found the solution, I cannot possibly return to the palace.

Thanks to the food Sujāhtā gave him, the prince recovered his spirits and left the forest of self-mortification.

Chapter 12
Enlightenment of Buddha

With renewed determination, Siddhārtha seated himself on a riverbank, under a bodhi tree.

I will not rise from here without attaining highest enlightenment!

The prince was determined to attain enlightenment or die.

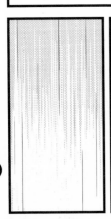

From then on a horde of demons appeared in the prince's mind, tempting him and seeking to overturn his resolve.

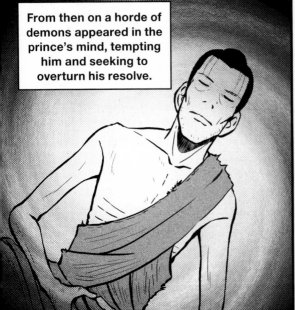

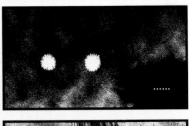

......

Your Highness . . .

You'll never attain enlightenment.

Give up! It's a lost cause.

You're wasting your time.

Why risk your life for something you'll never gain in a million years?

You're a fool.

It's beyond you.

If you had only stayed in the palace, you could have been king, and had a charmed life!

Your wife and child are waiting for you . . .

A happy family life can be yours . . .

Give it up!

Your Highness!

194

Don't undergo such needless torment. Come enjoy yourself with us.

We'll show you a good time, Your Highness!

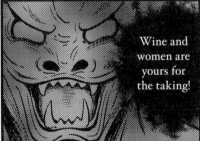

Wine and women are yours for the taking!

Grr

Siddhārtha, if you still won't give up, I'll have your life!

Kill him!!

195

Demons, be gone!!

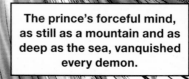

The prince's forceful mind,
as still as a mountain and as
deep as the sea, vanquished
every demon.

196

And then . . .

197

Prince Siddhārtha was 35 years old. This happened on December 8.

WHAT IS A BUDDHA?

The term "Buddha" refers to a being who has attained the highest level of enlightenment in the universe. There are countless Buddhas in the universe, but Prince Siddhārtha is the only being on earth ever to have attained that level of enlightenment. He was a prince of the Śākya clan, and so he is also referred to as "Śākyamuni Buddha."

In all, there are fifty-two levels of enlightenment. The highest level is known as "the enlightenment of Buddha." The word "enlightenment" (*satori*) refers to ultimate awareness of the universal truth that all people can attain true happiness.

To use a comparison from mountain climbing, the higher you climb, the more expansive a view you enjoy, until finally you attain the peak and you can see in all directions. In the same way, only someone who has attained the enlightenment of a Buddha can grasp the truth of the universe in its entirety. A being who has attained that level of enlightenment is known as a Buddha.

The teachings of Śākyamuni Buddha are what is known today as Buddhism.

I have attained all knowledge.
I have won victory over all.
I have achieved the eternal purpose!

As the morning star rose in the sky, the prince attained the highest level of enlightenment.

Prince Siddhārtha was 35 years old. This happened on December 8.

Chapter 13
The Wheel of Truth

The prince remained where he was for several weeks, enjoying the enlightenment of Buddha.

Ah . . .

The truth I have awakened to is extremely profound, far beyond the comprehension of people immersed in worldly pleasures.

They would not only fail to comprehend it, but even revile it.

Yet I must tell them.

I must tell all those who suffer, ignorant of life's meaning, about true happiness.

Very well.

First I will convey the truth to my former companions, Kauṇḍinya and the rest.

Buddha headed for the Deer Park.

206

Deer Park

Hey!

What is it?

The prince is on his way here.

What? Really?

207

Oh, His Highness is coming!

Don't call him that.

He is a good-for-nothing who gave up the rigors of fasting.

Everyone.

Life is suffering.

It is like a sea with ceaseless waves of suffering.

But we were not born to suffer, nor is that why we live.

Then why do we live? Can we not get through this life of tribulation in joy and gladness?

There is a way.

I have awakened to that truth.

In the heavens and on earth, only one sacred mission is ours.

Human beings can attain true happiness without fail.

Life has a purpose which, when attained, fills us with joy that we were born.

All people exist in order to enter this world of supreme bliss.

211

No matter how painful your life is . . .

. . . you must endure to the end, until you are saved into that happiness.

Before the blessed figure of the Buddha, the five men knelt.

And so Buddha began his first sermon.

This sermon is called "Setting in Motion the Wheel of Truth."

So began his 45 years of teaching, which lasted until he died at age 80, on February 15.

The teachings of those 45 years are what is known today as "Buddhism."

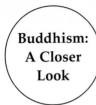

Buddhism: A Closer Look

Amida

Amida Buddha, the Buddha of infinite life and light. The greatest of all the Buddhas in the universe.

Primal Vow

The solemn promise made by Amida to save all humankind into absolute happiness without fail. Also known simply as the Vow.

Sutras

Sutras are sermons Buddha gave, transcribed by his disciples. All the teachings he gave from the age of thirty-five, when he attained enlightenment, until his death at the age of eighty have been written down. There are said to be over seven thousand sutras in all.

"In the heavens and on earth, only one sacred mission is ours."

Tenjo tenga yuiga dokuson (天上天下 唯我独尊): These words of the Buddha have often been misinterpreted to mean "I alone am great." Rather, they are a declaration of the existence of a sacred mission that only human beings, of all living things in the universe, can fulfill.

I must tell all those who are suffering, not knowing
the meaning of life, about true happiness.

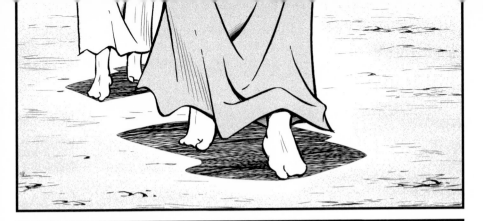

After he attained supreme enlightenment, Buddha traveled throughout India preaching.

Chapter 14
The Great Ship that Crosses the Sea of Life

People flocked to Buddha, their hearts absorbing the truth as dry land soaks up water.

He gained many disciples.

One day as he was preaching . . .

Ānanda

There is a great ship that can bear us across life's ceaseless waves of suffering, in joy.

What!

What does it mean to board the ship that crosses the sea of suffering?

It means that the root of suffering is destroyed, and we gain the great joy in life that exults "How glad I am that I was born human!"

But people do not know the true purpose of life. They are distracted by what is in front of their noses.

It is truly sad . . .

The purpose of life!

By what lies in front of their noses?

GULP

See the world for what it is.

Poor and rich,

old and young,

male and female.

All without exception suffer in pursuit of money and possessions.

224

If they have no land or house, they suffer to gain them.

If they have them, they suffer to maintain and supervise them.

Nor is that all.

Everything from honor and status to family and livestock, even clothing.

Those who lack them suffer, and so do those who have them.

It's true!

Those who have them are bound with chains of gold, those who do not with chains of iron.

Does anyone rejoice because the chains that bind him are made of gold?

225

......

No.

Of course not.

Whether the chains are made of gold or of iron, they cause suffering just the same.

Having and not having are one and the same.

The suffering of haves and have-nots is the same.

And yet people think "I suffer because I have no money." "I suffer because I have to guard my wealth." "I suffer because of my family."

Those things are not the root of suffering.

Where is the root of suffering?

It lies in your own darkness of mind.

Someone with a high fever cannot enjoy any delicacies.

Those whose hearts are in darkness cannot enjoy any happiness.

So unless you know the darkness of your mind and have it removed, you cannot attain true happiness.

I see . . .

It is Amida's Vow that destroys the root of suffering and gives us supreme happiness.

All people can be saved equally through the Primal Vow of Amida Buddha.

There is a world where every person's life can shine radiantly.

When the ultimate purpose of life is achieved, all suffering has its reward. Every tear returns to you a pearl.

Ah . . . Your Highness.

No . . . Buddha.

If you had not been born human . . .

. . . you could not have heard these truths.

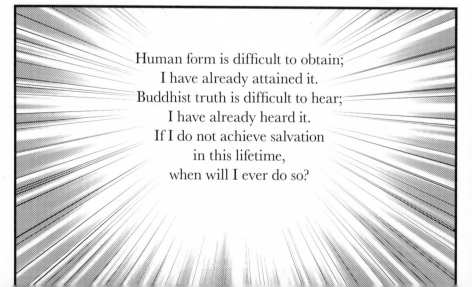

Human form is difficult to obtain;
I have already attained it.
Buddhist truth is difficult to hear;
I have already heard it.
If I do not achieve salvation
in this lifetime,
when will I ever do so?

Let me explain in more detail.

Human form is difficult to obtain;
I have already attained it.
Buddhist truth is difficult to hear;
I have already heard it.
If I do not achieve salvation
in this lifetime,
when will I ever do so?

234

The End

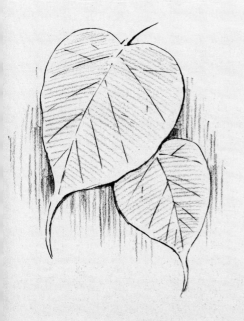

Afterword

I remember the messages of hope that a speaker heaped on us years ago at my junior high school graduation. "Kids, your future is bright. I want you to take wing, fly off to your hopes and dreams."

If we only could, my friends and I would be living ideal lives of perfect happiness. Instead we are full of uneasiness, despite the blessings of material abundance and technological advances.

In fact the entire world, despite drastically improved standards of living, seems to be in the grip of a fathomless anxiety. What happiness we have is vulnerable to events beyond our control: the prolonged economic downturn, natural catastrophes that strike without mercy, the threat of fearful new diseases . . .

Since childhood I myself have suffered from a troublesome illness that has burdened me with lifelong vague anxiety. As a young man I grappled with questions like "Life is so much trouble, so full of anxiety. Why do I have to live, anyway? What's it all for?" And I soon learned that the answers to these questions lie in Buddhism.

The deepening anguish that Prince Siddhārtha felt as he faced up to the realities of old age, sickness, and death is by no means an issue limited to the ancient past. This same anguish hits us today with unabated force. The story of Prince Siddhārtha's search for meaning and of his ultimate transformation reveals the unchanging nature of human life and the very purpose of our existence. Buddhism shows a profound truth, independent of time and place, that delivers us from despair into the light.

My own encounter with the teachings of Buddhism has brought me joy.

Now I have been given an opportunity to present the life of Buddha in graphic form.

I wrote this story hoping that readers would not dismiss it as mere biography or drama, but would find it relevant to real problems they face today.

But to portray the life of the greatest human the world has ever known was a daunting task, far beyond my powers. What enabled me to stay the course to the end was my close reading of the book *You Were Born for a Reason: The Real Purpose of Life* by Kentetsu Takamori, Daiji Akehashi, and Kentaro Ito. That book answers the age-old question, Why live?

I am extremely grateful to author Kentaro Ito for supervising the production of my book. Readers who want to learn about the meaning and purpose of life in greater depth are urged to turn to *You Were Born for a Reason*.

Hisashi Ota
July 2011

• • About the Author • •

HISASHI OTA
Born in Shimane Prefecture in 1970, he graduated from Nagoya
University's School of Science. His other works include *Manga
de wakaru bukkyo nyumon* (Understanding through Comics:
Introduction to Buddhism), which is forthcoming in English
from Ichimannendo Publishing, Inc.

Editorial supervisor:
KENTARO ITO, philosopher and co-author of *You Were Born for
a Reason: The Real Purpose of Life* published by Ichimannendo
Publishing, Inc.

Dear Reader,

Please take a minute to share your thoughts with us.

What made you stop to pick up our book at the bookstore?
How did you like the story of Buddha in Manga format?

Did this book have an impact on you? If so, how?

Your comments will be greatly appreciated in planning future titles.
Please email us at info@i-ipi.com

Or write us at Ichimannendo Publishing, Inc. (IPI),
970 W. 190th St., Suite 920, Torrance, CA 90502

For more information on this and other books by
Ichimannendo Publishing, Inc., please visit our website at
www.i-ipi.com

Ichimannendo Publishing, Inc.

YOU WERE BORN FOR A REASON
The Real Purpose of Life

By Kentetsu Takamori, Daiji Akehashi, and Kentaro Ito

What is the meaning of life? Where can we find true happiness that will never fade away? This book addresses these all-important questions head-on.

YOU WERE BORN FOR A REASON is the English translation of the runaway best-selling book on Buddhism, *Naze ikiru,* which has sold 600,000 copies since its publication in Japanese in 2001 and is still going strong.

List Price: $16.95 236 pages/Hardcover/9.3 x 6.3 inches ISBN 978-0-9790471-0-7

Something You Forgot ... Along the Way
Stories of Wisdom and Learning

By Kentetsu Takamori

This book introduces sixty-five heart-warming stories that show what it means to learn from life's events. These simple yet beautiful tales invite us to look deeper into almost any situation in life. In the tradition of Aesop's Fables each story concludes with a moral lesson.

This book was originally published in Japanese by Ichimannedo Publishing. It is part of a Japanese series which has sold over 1,000,000 copies.

List Price: $11.95 192 pages/Paperback/7.4 x 5.1 inches ISBN 978-0-9790471-1-4

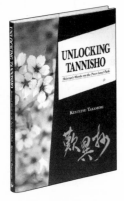

UNLOCKING TANNISHO
Shinran's Words on the Pure Land Path

By Kentetsu Takamori

Tannisho (Lamenting the Deviations) clarifies the heart of Pure Land Buddhism and points the way to real happiness with unforgettable expressions. *UNLOCKING TANNISHO* is the only definitive commentary of this beloved classic text, and has been a remarkable success with 200,000 copies sold to date.

List Price: $30.00 144 pages/Hardcover/10 x 7 inches ISBN 978-0-9790471-5-2